Brentwood

in old picture postcards

by
Frank D. Simpson

Third edition

European Library - Zaltbommel/Netherlands MCMLXXXV

Cover picture:
The western end of High Street about 1908 at its junction with Kings Road (right) and Weald Lane (left) before they were widened. The three small properties on the left were demolished for this purpose by 1930 and replaced with two shops with offices and a doctors' surgery above. The Institute on the right was not taken down until much later. The garage sign points the way to Brentwood's first motor garage of Johnstone Brothers located where Bennett's funeral establishment now stands. The horse waggonette on the left and the baker's cart complete the animated summer scene.

GB   ISBN 90 288 3053 7 / CIP

European Library in Zaltbommel/Netherlands publishes among other things the following series:

IN OLD PICTURE POSTCARDS *is a series of books which sets out to show what a particular place looked like and what life was like in Victorian and Edwardian times. A book about virtually every town in the United Kingdom is to be published in this series. By the end of this year about 175 different volumes will have appeared. 1,250 books have already been published devoted to the Netherlands with the title* **In oude ansichten.** *In Germany, Austria and Switzerland 500, 60 and 15 books have been published as* **In alten Ansichten;** *in France by the name* **En cartes postales anciennes** *and in Belgium as* **En cartes postales anciennes** *and/or* **In oude prentkaarten** *150 respectively 400 volumes have been published.*

For further particulars about published or forthcoming books, apply to your bookseller or direct to the publisher.

This edition has been printed and bound by Grafisch Bedrijf De Steigerpoort in Zaltbommel/Netherlands.

INTRODUCTION

Though I cannot claim to be a true Brentwoodian by birth, for I was just three years old when my parents came to the town in 1913, all my upbringing was in Brentwood and my schooling obtained at the Grammar School (as the present Brentwood School was then always known), I feel I can at least claim to be an Old Brentwoodian in that capacity.

I lived and worked in Brentwood for forty-five years during which time I acquired an affection for the place and its environment which has remained with me ever since. Over the years I gathered a quantity of old picture postcards and photographs of the district and some of local events which have travelled with me to wherever I have lived since, and I can say that I have never tired of turning over the leaves of my album from time to time. Distance, age and the fact that no longer does any member of the family reside in the district now regretfully precludes more than a very occasional fleeting visit.

A number of the postcards were kindly given to me, or loaned to me for copying by residents who knew or shared my interest for which I have been ever grateful. I have always cherished the hope that some day it would be possible for others to share in the enjoyment these old postcards have given me. Happily, the European Library has provided me with the opportunity to make a selection of scenes from my collection for publication, this little book being the result.

My earliest recollections of the town are of the 1914-1918 war period when our then rather quiet country town was quickly transformed into one vast garrison – not only on account of the great military establishment at Warley, now no more, but also because a military camp was set up on Shenfield Common and the Highwood Hospital was occupied by the military, and the Poplar schools (now the Hutton Residential School) became the temporary home of the Duke of York's School evacuated from Dover, and almost every household had one or more soldiers billeted upon them. Army mule-waggons appeared to be everywhere and motor

ambulances, some fitted with balloon like containers carried on the roof, which enabled them to operate on town-gas, could often be seen as several of the large houses around the town were converted into military hospitals and war injured soldiers in 'hospital blue' became a common sight in the town.

There were very few motor vehicles then, only an occasional lorry or steam hauled vehicle was to be seen: almost everything that did not travel by the railway was horse-drawn or manually propelled. The gentry could be seen in their carriages with a coachman or groom, gigs, dog-carts or pony-traps were the usual mode of conveyance for the less opulent who lived out of town: the bicycle or 'Shank's Pony' sufficed for all others. Almost every shopkeeper had his delivery cart or van or an errand boy who rode a carrier cycle or perambulated a barrow or handcart for deliveries. The motor-bus was still unknown though there was one small horse-drawn closed conveyance which was known locally as the 'fever box' because it closely resembled the vehicle used for taking patients to the isolation hospital at Billericay, which trundled somewhat sorrowfully between the railway station, the town and Herongate two or three times daily until 1920 when the first motor-buses arrived in the town. From this time forward the automobile has steadily ousted the horse until we have now reached the point where it completely dominates our whole existence.

Since the coming of the Eastern Counties Railway in 1840 the development of the town has been almost exclusively of a residential character. No single industrial activity has ever been a major factor in the life of the district. This is due chiefly to its favourable location at a convenient distance from the Metropolis for commuting daily. The healthy atmosphere and elevated situation besides attracting former London residents has also brought a number of hospitals and similar establishments into the district. These, coupled with the service, distributive and ancillary trades have been the chief providers of employment in the town: though brick-making and the agricultural machinery works of Burgess & Company deserve mention. Other factors favourable to the growth of the town are the beautiful open spaces or commons which escaped enclosure such as Shenfield and Childerditch: the goodly number of large private estates and parks which happily still remain – some in public ownership for pleasure uses – though in other cases their usage has changed. The schools too have saved much land from the hands of the builders, and preserved a number of fine houses which otherwise could not have survived, particularly near the town centre. This has done much to break up that continuous and monotonous growth of 'bricks and mortar' which many other dormitory towns now have to endure.

Until the telephone came into general use, the postcard was the accepted medium of communication for all manner of purposes where a short non-confidential message required transmission. It was cheap, twopence (pre-decimal) would buy a packet of five pictorial views which cost but one half-penny each for postage until about 1917 when it rose to one penny, though a five word greeting could still be sent at the old charge. The business world also found great use for the postcard; it was used by customers for sending in orders or for acknowledgement of the same and for advice of despatch: commercial travellers never failed to acquaint their anticipated places of call by sending a postcard stating the date and time of the next intended visit, and they saw extensive use for advertising purposes. Except for sending a 'Wish you were here' or similar message from those on vacation the postcard has, sad to say, now practically vanished from every day usage.

The world today owes an enormous debt to those pioneer producers of postcards – their photographers have left us a rich heritage of inestimable value: many of the views and scenes they captured for us of a bygone age would otherwise have never been recorded and made so readily available for later generations. Many of the old railway companies were also responsible for producing picture postcards in vast numbers extolling the beauty and objects of interest in the territories they served, which today are now collectors' items as indeed many other postcards are now becoming.

Selecting the cards to give the broadest aspect within the space available has not been easy, so I have endeavoured to avoid using the better known subjects which feature more frequently in magazines and similar publications, and have also largely eschewed church views for no other reason than that they get used a great deal, and happily are the most enduring and unchanging edifices in our environment.

The cards have been arranged mainly as though the viewer has been taken on a contemporary perambulation of the town and district commencing at the railway station, then proceeding up to the town to follow a fairly logical itinerary, complementary views have where possible been placed in juxtaposition for ease of comparison. Because newer residents of the town may have some difficulty in identifying the precise location of some now vanished premises, the street numbers concerned have been quoted in the captions to the postcards.

It is hoped that this little collection may stimulate past memories and some nostalgia among older viewers and also that the younger generation may gather something of how the town has developed from the time when 'grandma' stepped out to go shopping, or perhaps took a quiet walk with 'grandpapa' through some of the pleasant ways which then abounded. Others may perhaps feel obliged to take a closer look at parts of the town to see how much of the past still remains identifiable.

I have made no attempt to deal with the early history of the town, this has already been done by far more competent hands than mine.

1. To begin this little book on a light note here is Ye Old Brentwood Tramp's Band which played in the annual carnival or at similar events to raise funds for local charities. It flourished until 1914, and attempts were made after the war to revive it, many of its former members did not return from the war and it soon faded away. It is photographed at the rear of the Railway Hotel. The gentleman who supplied the card was unable to identify which of the players was himself! This is not surprising when one looks at the heavy disguises adopted.

2. Brentwood and Warley railway station about the turn of the century, the site for the development of Rose Valley and Alexandra Road is being cleared. The high building in the trees is the former Industrial School, later it was Hibbards furniture warehouse and saleroom, recently demolished. The original signal-box is on the platform in the foreground where timber is being prepared for a new footbridge to connect the platforms, passengers hitherto having to walk across the rails. The bow roof of the engine shed can be seen at the end of the platform. As yet no building has commenced on the Cornsland Estate in the background.

Brentwood Station. (G. E. R)

3. A later view card of almost the same location: the houses in lower Rose Valley and Alexandra Road are now completed and the road is made up. This also shows the 'up' platform with its little belfry; until 1 July 1900 the bell was rung a few minutes before every train departure. The roof of the engine shed has been renewed for a gable type and the end of the new footbridge can be seen (bottom right); four cabs stand on the station forecourt where a new shelter for the drivers has arrived. There is still no building at Cornslands.

4. Proceeding towards the town, on the right is the Railway Tavern at the junction of Kings Road with King Edward Road whilst still in the ownership of Hill's Brentwood brewery (see card 77), to the rear is Ellis's carriage building shop with forge and wheelwright shop, left is Arnold's mens clothier, later Stokes followed by Caton and then a D.I.Y. store: these have now all gone, the site covered by Ewing House. Notice the stone cobbles laid for foot passengers to cross the road which appears to be in a dreadful state. The Railway Tavern is now transferred across the road near where the Railway Hotel once stood.

Queen's Road, Brentwood   No. 369

5. Now a little farther up the hill this card of circa 1927 shows the junction of Kings Road (left) with Queens Road and Gresham Road (right), the two shops have recently been demolished for new development, were then Holland's café and Gutteridge the baker and post office: left is the garden of The Shrubbery, home of the Fielder family who owned the brewery (see card 55): later the lower part of the garden became Rendle's Garden Centre. Note the old sign indicating there was a public telephone inside the post office.

Brentwood, Queens Road.

6. Now near the top of Queens Road about 1910 looking west, since when the scene has not changed significantly. The large house with twelve chimneys, known as St. Mildred's which housed the telephone exchange for many years, has now been replaced. At this time the Spread Eagle public house was owned by Smith Garrett's Bow Brewery, passing later to Taylor Walker before coming to Ind Coope more recently. The little railed enclosure in front has long been taken away: notice the stand-pipe with swivel for filling the water carts for sprinkling the streets in dry weather.

7. Now turned into Ingrave Road towards the cross road, this early card shows the school chapel, the old school room and the master's house. Notice the immense size of the martyr's tree before it was enclosed with an iron railing; left are the three sister limes which were planted circa 1820, now only two remain though much larger. Almost all the scholars, anxious to get in the picture, wear mortar-board hats — the day of the Eton collar had not yet come, the suits are very varied. The head of a master can be seen peeping over the wall to the right.

Ingrave Road. Brentwood

132053

8. This card taken a few yards west and fifty years later than the last at the time when many buses took lay-over in Ingrave Road at the point where the new Hambro Road has been made: from the left the first and last are Hillman's famous coaches to Bow, second is an 'Old Tom' from Laindon, next a London General for Stratford, and fourth is Simpson's bus from Leaden Roding which ran to Dunmow. Of the shops facing, the one left of the tree is Maddison's coffee shop, he founded the pioneer holiday camp at Caister Norfolk; right is Rogers hairdressing saloon and the sister lime trees are on the right.

9. Still in Ingrave Road looking toward Ongar Road. Here is the original Wilson's Store still not quite complete which was destroyed by fire in 1909 which was replaced by the fine building (now Cooper's). The white gates and coach house (right) belong to The Hollies where Miss Duchesne for many years conducted her select academy for gentlemen's daughters until the 1930's when it moved to St. Thomas's Road.

10. This card of circa 1906 shows the cross road looking toward Shenfield: left is Corner House, for many years home of the Lewis family, which was reconstructed about 1928 into a bank with two shops and chambers above. To the right is Old House, the white house was Mrs. Saville's sweet shop until replaced by Eadena House. The ivy covered building was the office of Landon's solicitors since rebuilt as Landon House with flats above. An early automobile stands outside and the boys are obviously very interested in the photographer.

BRENTWOOD MARTYR'S MEMORIAL

11. The cross road looking west on a card of the late 1890's showing the newly completed row of shops on the right (1-23) which replaced some very dilapidated property (see card No. 13). The old Wilson building is on the left, the tall brick house remained in its burnt out state following the great fire for about forty years because of a dispute between the parties on either side.

12. A reversed view to No. 11 at about the same date showing the original Wilson emporium with its high mansard roof: right is the Mansion House recently restored by an insurance company for offices, now the sole survivor of the several fine houses that adorned the street, it was the home and surgery of Dr. Quennell. Next is the White Horse Inn, now modernised, beyond a butcher shop and three houses recently demolished for new shops and offices. Behind the brougham stood the large pump used by waggoners until the stone trough and drinking fountain was built near the signpost.

13. An early card of High Street looking east showing the old property replaced by the new parade (see previous view) and the first 'Yorkshire Grey' soon after rebuilt, see No. 14, the tiny white shop survived until circa 1930 of Mary Ann Twinn, an eccentric who left everything in the window as her mother left them many years before. It was festooned with cobwebs, sweets had melted in the jars and all was thick with dust of ages.

14. This card shows the reconstructed Yorkshire Grey; it was altered later when a balcony replaced the verandah and a refreshment room opened at the right with an entrance through the window next to the flagpole. The old cab or 'growler', the title more usually bestowed upon them, is no doubt from Culver's jobmasters establishment two doors to the left of the inn, in what is now known as Doone's yard after Mr. Doone who took over the business replacing the cabs with motor taxis and hire cars. New shops now cover the site of this once well known land mark: the forecourt was taken for a public convenience.

High Street, Brentwood. 143876

15. The same area as shown on a postcard of about 1930, the position of the Yorkshire Grey is indicated by its lofty sign board and the white wall of the public convenience. There is a fine selection of vintage motors including an Austin 16 saloon, behind it is a motorcycle and sidecar with acetylene lighting, next a Dodge saloon with an old Reo bus behind: Mr. Curtis's red and white Ongar & District bus is just leaving. Next an original first type Morris 8, and finally an Eastern National Gilford coach. The Arcade (right) has replaced the County Motor Works of Mr. Good which followed Percy Crowe's mens outfitting shop.

16. Now in St. Thomas's Road, this view from the church gate about 1908 shows the 1896 post office at far end on left, the garden on right is now covered by the Arcade and earlier by Rippons Garage. Most of the houses have now become offices: for many years the Brentwood Gazette was produced in the last house on the right. Facing the camera in High Street is another fine house, 'Red House', where Woolworths' new store stands: previously Bakers' Fashions and two other shops.

17. Returned to the High Street: this early view is probably from the same camera as No. 11 but a little farther west. Only one building of all those shown here still stands today, the three storey property on the right (Nos. 22-24), left is the Manor House, right was The Laurels, a fine double bay windowed house where Tesco is now. Next was a seedmens shop and nursery, now occupied by the post office. The trees left were removed when the new trees were planted along the whole of this end of the street. How wide and spacious it all seems without traffic.

18. This is High Street looking west from the same point as No. 17 a few years later after kerbs and paving flags have been laid; the first two shops on the right (Nos. 53-55) became Boots Chemists, the next two were taken down and rebuilt for Mac Fisheries and Sainsbury's. Left the first shop is Smith's corn stores (later Gramphorn's) followed by a house and the Chequers Hotel with its pair of gables and white stucco front, next the low wall in front of the Priory (a private house) and the chapel ruins. The large chimneys on the right belonged to the Lion and Lamb Hotel before it was rebuilt.

High Street, Brentwood. 96928.

19. This 1928 card clearly shows the changed appearance of the scene in the last card, which also includes the Palace, the town's first cinema made from Charter's old drapery shop to include two small lock-ups and still retaining the original fascia. Next come the new shops mentioned at card No. 18: left, the house is now Cullen's grocery taken later by Mence Smith. The Chequers now has a red brick frontage. Notice the old fashioned hinged canvas sunblinds on the cycle shop (right). The current film at the Palace is 'The Chess Player'.

20. This card of about 1910 is a fine front view of the Manor House, on the left in No. 17. It was the home of Mr. John Quennell, a local solicitor in partnership with Mr. C.E. Lewis. He was Clerk to the Justices and Registrar of the County Court for many years. The house was taken down about 1937 and shops and flats built on its site, Lloyds Bank occupying the right-hand end.

HIGH STREET, BRENTWOOD from the Air

21. A fine aerial view of central High Street area in the late 1920's: bottom centre is the former Town Hall (now Courts furnishers), opposite is the Gas Office, five blocks to the right is the White Hart with its old white plaster front, next is the Midland Bank just above which are the little houses of Cottage Place, demolished circa 1934 to make way for the Electric showrooms. North Road Avenue and the Debtors' Field are at the top. The new Chapel High stands where the clump of trees are, and nearly opposite is the white roof of the Palace Cinema: Crown Street is bottom right. The number of old sheds or barns at the rear of the main premises is remarkable, they were seldom seen by the general public.

22. An 1890 view of middle High Street identifiable by the Westminster, at that time London County Westminster and Parr's Bank on the left. On the right after the second shop are the small shops taken down for a new Essex Bank, now Barclay's. Notice the small windows in David Rist's grocery on the right and in Crowe's china and furniture shop next along: the subsequent alterations to these properties as shown in the next card are worthy of close examination.

23. Another card from almost the same location reveals considerable modernisation has taken place at most of the shops; most notable is the substitution of plate glass— then coming into fashion – for the old small windows and the use of numerous gas lights in large glass globes for shop window illumination outside. Notice the display of gentlemen's boots outside Mr. Fuller's shop, the most expensive is 8/11 or 45p today! This shop passed to D.C. Smith and then Bata. David Rist's is now the International and Isaac Rist, across the street, was taken by the London Cooperative. Next to it is J.J. Crowe's drapery and shoe shop, the new bank is on the right.

Thomas a Beckett Chapel, Brentwood.

24. Diverting left into the north end of the Chapel High taken from part of New Road where are the remains of the thirteenth century chapel which had fallen into a ruinous state after building the present parish church. In 1902 Squire Tower of Weald Hall was instrumental in getting the remains made safe, tidied up and enclosed as shown on this contemporary card. The building right is part of The Priory, a private house erected on the site of the chaplain's house. This was demolished to provide the site for the Odeon cinema and its garden became the car park. All this has in turn been cleared to create the present Chapel High shopping centre.

25. Passing through the Chapel High to the remaining section of New Road, which formerly continued through to the High Street, are the County Court and Congregational Church, both photographed here before the Church House and Technical School were built on the open land. Both have now been removed and their place taken by the new clinic. The wooden building on the left was part of the premises forming the Queen Inn which also no longer exists. Until the Court House etc., was built in London Road, the County Court building served also as the police court and offices of solicitors Lewis and Quennell.

Brentwood, Crown Street

26. Returning to High Street by way of Crown Street passing the multi-storey car park which occupies the site of the villas and Abbey Lodge, shown on the left. The tree disappeared many years ago. The gates on the right mark the entry to Regency Court built in the grounds of 'Gweedore', home of Mr. J.J. Crowe (mentioned earlier), who took a deep interest in local civic matters. For many years his two daughters ran Gweedore P N E U School for young children which stood in the garden, entered from Primrose Hill.

27. Facing north from almost the same spot as the last view. The buildings on the right suffered considerable damage from enemy action in the last war: the opening by Larkins shop, which still trades under that name, is the new entry to South Street which has changed dramatically in recent years. A mobile ice-cream vendor is approaching in his pony drawn vehicle adapted from a small governess-car. The White Hart Hotel is just visible in the distance.

28. This 1920 card shows the scene on emerging from Crown Street looking to the north side of High Street. The large ironmongery store (left) is now the Midland Bank; next in order are Home & Colonial Stores, Buckle & Blake (grocery); the next pair and the opening to Cottage Place formed the site for the electric showrooms. Then three more shops and Barclay's Bank recently re-fronted. The roof of the three tall shops was used for many years for the Fire Brigade Escape Rescue competition, an annual event which was eagerly awaited by the town children.

29. This view is about ninety-five years ago. The White Hart is on the right, the very narrow entry to Crown Street is on the left, the high clap-boarded property of Carter the grocer was pulled down to improve the width of the road, as was the old Kings Head and a forge on the other corner. A new Kings Head was built farther back from the street, and a fish shop was in front where the Nationwide offices now stand. The sign of the former George and Dragon can be seen on the left. Notice the fine three dimensional sign on the White Hart. The vehicle in the foreground appears to be a shell fish cart, the man on the left is carrying his wares on a wooden tray under his arm.

30. This card, which may be dated about 1900, is taken slightly west of the last. The first shop left is on the site of the old Kings Head (No. 80), next is a wool shop, then Silver's Café, formerly the first International Stores, followed by the Town Hall. On the right the butcher's shop was divided to become a surgery and a builders office. The next was Newman, the saddler, taken by Lipton's, followed by Worrin, a chemist, which became the Gas Office. The next small shop by the posting box was the post office until the first Crown office opened in 1896.

High Street, Brentwood.

31. The photographer of this card is outside the Town Hall in 1930, of which Evelyn's shop was part. The next three shops were earlier the private house of the Wallis's whose shop has just closed and is up for sale. The vehicles are of interest, there are two flat radiator Morris-Cowleys, an early Austin 7 tourer, and a little Singer van. The omnibus is a Westcliff A E C Reliance going to Southend. First shop on right is Marsh, outfitter, followed by Wallis's hardware and Wilson & Whitworth's, the printers, with the sun blind in front.

High Street Brentwood.

32. This view of about 1906 is a little lower down and facing east. Left is the fine old Swan Inn which was replaced by a new one about 1935. On the right is J.T. Humphrey's pawnbroking establishment with its sign of the three golden balls. Most of the shops mentioned in No. 31 are to be seen on the left, next to the Swan is the tailor's shop of S.H. Taylor, who is looking out of his door with an apprentice probably interested in the sight of an early automobile approaching.

33. A 1908 card of the former Bell Inn, property of Wells & Perry's Chelmsford brewery, taken over by Taylor Walker about 1930 and taken down some years ago when new shops were erected farther back to provide a wider pavement which was very narrow at this point. The site is now in the occupation of 'Good Sense' (fashions), the Essex Trustee Savings Bank and Rumbelows Electrical.

34. From a card of 1912 showing 137-139 High Street which faced Kings Road. These were taken down about sixty years ago to improve the entrance to Weald Lane. Dean's shop was not replaced, two new shops with a surgery and offices over were built on the site, the dairy and tobacconist moved lower down to Nos. 143-145. H. Foley, who has just taken over the dairy from Wm. Guess, is obviously proud of his new milk float — a good example of this specialised type of vehicle once a familiar sight on the streets. S. Horne, who was newsagent as well as tobacconist, was a familiar figure around the town crying his evening papers he collected off the train.

35. This card of circa 1900 is very similar to the cover picture, it reveals the original Sir Charles Napier which was rebuilt farther back at the same time as the shops were demolished in the last view. The sign of The Bell and the Town Hall clock are to be seen on the right and Burgess's wine shop which had passed to A.J. Hazell in the later view. The three little girls with the perambulator seem far more concerned with what the photographer is doing than with the possibility of being in the way of any traffic. Kings Road is on the right with the corner of The Institute just in view.

36. Now part of Western Gardens, this old card shows the white-washed cottages known as 'Stone Yard' though the correct address was North Street. The cottages continued round the corner along Western Road and then into Weald Road, and were all cleared at the time of the road improvement, after which the site became a car park for some years. One old man kept a donkey in the tiny yard at the back of his cottage which he brought in and out daily through the house and the front door! The flank wall left bounded Drake's bakery and garden on which the first houses forming Western Gardens were built.

HACKNEY INSTITUTION, BRENTWOOD, from the Air

37. Another of the aerial views of the 1920's showing the Hackney homes for epileptics, now St. Faith's Hospital. Left is the town cemetery, bottom centre is the newly opened Anglo-American (now Esso) Oil Coy's distribution depot, built on part of the old brickfield. Right is the La Plata estate where Hubert Road, the Court House, Police Station and houses now stand. La Plata was originally known as Westbury Lodge. It was built by a Mr. Dearsley, the last occupier being Mrs. De Pinna.

38. Few will recognise the location of this card of the junction of London Road Brook Street with Spital Lane about ninety years ago, with the village general shop — later Gilbert the butcher. Next is the long delicensed King William IV beerhouse, beyond which is the range of buildings acquired by J.P. Hensmans for his Ford Motor showrooms. Here also he kept his fleet of purple Sunset coaches which operated between Brentwood and Charing Cross until compulsorily acquired by the London Transport Board in 1934 after enjoying great popularity with commuters who paid 10/- (50p) for a weekly ticket.

Brook Street, Brentwood.

39. Brook Street village looking east about 1930. Spital Lane is left just beyond Hensman's motor showroom and Mascall's Lane is opposite. Left is the Bull Inn, an old roadside hostelry outside which a man who was examining a horse with a view to purchase had his ear bitten off. At this time the land on the right was occupied by the yard and stables of a cartage contractor, the Kit-Cat transport café and the forge and blacksmith's shop belonging to Mr. Wingrave, his family having worked it throughout from the sixteenth century. The very large telegraph poles were removed a year or so later.

40. Brook Street a little further west at the same date as the previous card, the Bull Inn in the distance. It would be difficult to attach any more advertising to Turret House which is also the post office. Piccadilly cigarettes were 4d (less than 2p) for 10! None of the six brands advertised here are obtainable today. Note the old type concrete telephone kiosk and the newspaper contents bills which ceased with paper rationing in 1939 and have not appeared since.

41. Here is a splendid view of the Golden Fleece taken in 1896, happily it still retains many of its characteristics. The Homesteads estate has not yet been started. The infant Ingrebourne River passes under the road in the dip to join Weald Brook away to the left where there was at one time a water mill; the Moat House stands behind the trees on the right. A few hens appear to be pecking about near the waggon where they will find grains dropped from the horses nosebags. The XVII milestone from London is near the top of the hill.

Weald Road. South Weald.   128017.

42. A view in Weald Road looking towards the town from near the Halfway House Farm where the new dual carriage way byepass passes beneath. The tall building over the trees is St. Charles' School which has now become a juvenile remand home. This road has long been a favourite walk for Brentwood folk to South Weald village and the park which has now become public.

South Weald, Weald Hall Belvedere

43. The Belvedere in Weald Park about 1900. It was built by Thomas Tower Esq. after purchasing the estate in the late eighteenth century. It was a romantic embattled square tower with bevelled corners. Originally it was known as the Prospect House enabling its owner to overlook much of his property. In recent times the fabric had deteriorated to the point of becoming unsafe, so was taken down, though its approaches still remain.

44. This old postcard shows the former Wheelers' Arms which still exists as a private house. It was a small beer house of Fielders Brewery, and is in Wheelers Lane which links Coxtie Green Road and Navestock Side, and perpetuating a name which would otherwise have been long forgotten as it lost its license about sixty years ago.

45. This is a typical Essex timber framed and weather boarded building from a postcard of about 1898. It is the King William the Fourth in Tan House Lane at Navestock when George Furlong was the landlord. The front garden and hedge have now all been taken to form a car park in front. Seated outside is a real Essex worthy wearing the regular black knitted cardigan jacket over dark grey whipcord waistcoat and trousers with hard hat. Notice also his stick which has been cut from a hedge.

46. A fine view of Pilgrims Hall at Pilgrims Hatch, a good example of Victorian elegance with covered balcony/verandah, and a quiet game of croquet in progress when Dale Womersley Esq., who was a noted sportsman, was owner. Earlier a boarding academy for young gentlemen was conducted here by Alexander Watson. It passed later to J.F.N. Lawrence, who was one of the Governors of Brentwood School and a Chairman of the Justices. Notice the fox weathervane on the lantern which had a repeater inside the house. It is now a Fellowship House.

47. Returning to town via Ongar Road, the first building for many years was the Robin Hood & Little John public house, seen here about 1900, with, just beyond the first five shops hereabouts newly completed. There are still empty building sites and nothing is on the right below the new Highwood Hospital wall, and no pavements have yet been laid. For many years R. White & Co. of mineral water fame had a depot and stables here, bulk supplies being brought from London by steam wagon. Local deliveries were by a fine pair horse cart, the jingle of the trace chains and of the glass ball stoppered bottles made a pleasant accompaniment to the clip-clop of the horses hoofs along the streets.

Brentwood, Ongar Road.

48. A little farther along the same road. This card, which was posted in 1907, has, apart from the dreadful condition of the road and paths, and vacant plots (where there are hedges still), not changed very materially in the interim. Tiffin's coaches and taxis are garaged on the right near the top next to a house that was formerly Franklin's Britannia photographic studio.

49. This pre-1912 card shows yet another vanished Brentwood public house: it is the former Rising Sun, the present building stands in what was the garden at the rear of the one pictured here. The ground on the right is now part of Western Avenue, formed about 1929. The old footpath across the Pennyloaf fields to Western Road is clearly visible, here again there was no footpath or kerbing at this date.

Brentwood. Burland Road.

50. Few of today's Brentwood residents would ever believe that Burland Road could ever have looked as it does in this pre-1914 view card, or perhaps a little earlier. Only the first two houses appear to have been built. The meadow on the right formed part of the Victoria Works and land (see next card). It was used for experiments and testing of motor mowers of which some few were manufactured until the works closed down about the end of 1922.

BURGESS & KEY'S
REAPING MACHINE MANUFACT

BRENTWOOD,—ESSEX.

51. This card, which is unfortunately imperfect, has been made from a trade card, but no other view of the Victoria Works has yet come to light. The business began in mid-Victorian days by a Mr. Burgess with Sir Reuben Key to make reaping machines of which they were pioneers. Later it traded as W.J. & C.T. Burgess & Co. The invention of the patented self-binder in America practically killed this side of the business, and though hay presses, cotton gins and latterly motor mowers were introduced, its old prosperity was never regained. The buildings were taken over about 1923 by A.E. Symes Ltd., a large London building contractor. This view is from the corner of North Road; note the pond.

Ongar Road Brentwood.

52. The top end of Ongar Road as it used to be; the Castle Inn aside, little else now remains. Shops have replaced the cottages Nos. 1-15 right; the Victoria Works occupied the land from the Castle Inn to Burland Road. Left, all has been cleared as far as the houses behind the poplar trees in front of Hagon's builders yard, later Henderson's garage, to make the entrance in 1938 to the City Coach Co's head office (now Thermos) and depot (now Eastern National) in 1952. The railings left were in front of the old Drill Hall, now in process of conversion to an indoor shopping centre after previous use as a warehouse for Eade's Ltd.

53. This pre-1912 view of the top end of Weald Road, as seen from the land where the Council houses now stand, includes another long vanished Brentwood public house: the Spotted Dog, kept in its later years by Harry Simmons, who was also a cartage contractor, with tip carts used by the Council and local builders. The alley way leading through to Tower Hill can be seen between the first house and Simmons gates.

54. View from near the junction of Weald Lane with Tower Hill looking towards South Weald. In the background to the right is the lane which is now Park Road before any houses had been built. The land on the left is now covered by the houses in Sir Frances Way and on the right is Bardswell Close. The photographer placed himself on top of the bank where the last of the Council houses now stand.

Kings Road looking over Warley. 40.

55. This postcard, which was posted in 1924, is of much earlier date because the Baptist Church, which was built in 1915, stands where the wooden photographic studio can be seen on the corner of Chase Road, now Kings Chase, which is now also built over. On the left is Fielder's brewery and opposite is a pantile roofed property always known as the Shanty which was an upholsterers for many years. Visiting fairs and circuses used the vacant land, hence the name Fairfield Road where the Council houses were built. The brewery was converted into shops, but the Brewery Tap is still there on the corner of Primrose Hill.

56. Here is Lower Kings Road about 1900. On the left is Sinclair's leather and saddlery shop, Robinson's retail corn stores — his grinding and provender mill across the road. Next are Bowtell, plumber and decorator, and other small shops. The Parade branches to the left where the bridge approach commences. None of these premises exist today. See also the next two cards.

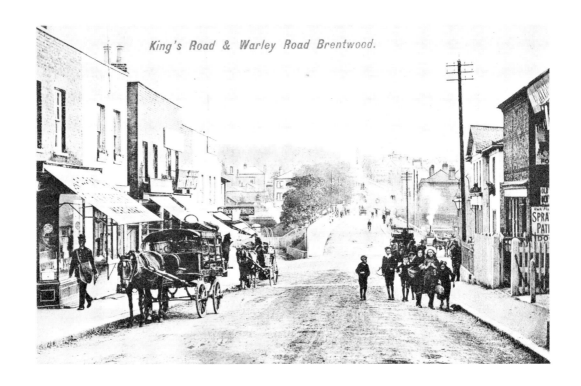

King's Road & Warley Road Brentwood.

57. A later view of almost the same area as in the last card in which Robinson's mill (later Matthews) and the Railway Hotel — between which the entry to Railway Square formerly went — can be seen more clearly. These buildings have all been swept away, and shops, offices and a new Railway Tavern now cover the site. The front greengrocery cart is from Baverstock's shop on the right over the bridge. The other cart belongs to Mr. Gilder in the same line of business, who travelled the town for many many years.

58. A later view showing the new station building erected when the line to Shenfield was doubled. Part of The Parade and the Parade Cinema are on the left, and right is the London Cooperative Society's coal office and the council yard all of which have now gone for new development. On the right stands the new Pegasus House behind which is a vast car park where the goods depot formerly lay. Palmer the boot repairer, in the white apron, would re-sole gentlemens boots for 3/3d (now 16p) or heel them for 1/3d (6p). Notice all the trees in the last view have gone.

BRENTWOOD . 804.

Fred Spalding
Photo
Chelmsford
Copyright

59. Passing over the bridge this 1908 card shows the original station entrance on the 'up' side which White in 1848 described as 'one of the handsomest of the smaller stations on the Eastern Counties Railway' which opened in 1840. This was demolished to make way for the widening which had been mentioned already. The station staff are well aware of the presence of the photographer. On the left over the station can be seen the Hunter Memorial Hall which has seen a variety of uses. A terrace of shops is now on the left where the trees stood.

Warley Road, Brentwood No. 388

60. The lower part of Warley Hill at the point where Avenue Road branches to the right which may be dated a little after 1920 by the old Ford taxicab ascending the hill. The buildings are still very similar, though the Wesleyan chapel has been modernised in front, in course of which it lost its rather elegant pinnacles. Cramphorns mill, on the left, is now a warehouse for office supplies.

61. One wonders how all the public houses made a living in the past, for this is another that closed its doors many years ago. It is The Brass Bar, so named from the brass hitching rail on the front of the building which is not without architectural interest aided by the small ornamental balcony. It became a fish and chip shop, and more recently a house with car sales adjoining.

WARLEY MENTAL HOSPITAL, BRENTWOOD from the Air

62. This is another in the series of aerial views of the town which are very helpful in getting sight of properties not normally visible to the average citizen. This gives an excellent impression of the great extent of buildings and land at Warley Hospital, formerly the Essex County Lunatic Asylum. It was built largely on land which formed part of the Brentwood Hall Estate, home of the Kavanagh family. Top left is the old Brentwood Gas Works, top centre is Crescent Road with Warley Hill and Junction Road just below it at top right. The houses in Chase Road can be seen just above the large gas-holder.

Headley Arms Great Warley near Brentwood.

63. The present Headley Arms bears little resemblance to its predecessor shown here in this pretty setting of about seventy years ago. It takes its name from a former Lord of the Manor: Lord Headley of the Allanson-Winn family. The title is held today by Charles Rowland, who is the seventh Baron, but is also the thirteenth Baronet of Nostell and the seventh of Little Warley, creations of 1797, 1660 and 1776 respectively, of Aghadoe Co Kerry and Arundel Sussex.

64. Across the small Headley Commom, on the west side of the Tilbury Road, lies the Great Ropers estate – home of the Hirst family for generations. It is, in fact, in South Weald parish. This early card fails to reveal why the family are so disposed on one of its several lawns. The semi-circular bays and pedimented front entrance of this fine house are of interest. The house takes its name from Henry Roper, pursuivant to Katherine of Aragon, who let the lands in 1617 to William Ipgrave from whom they passed to John Hirst.

65. Separated from the last property by Green Lane was the Warley Place estate; the house depicted here was the home of that great horticulturist and eccentric Ellen Willmott, who evolved or collected many new varieties of plants – many to this day bearing the sub-title Willmottii. She expended a considerable fortune creating several very specialised gardens employing up to sixty gardeners at one time, to the detriment of the main property. After her death in the late 1930's the property was sold, and the house completely demolished. The War delayed the proposed development, which has however been disallowed. The large open area is a delightful sight when the millions of spring bulbs are in bloom.

The Thatchers Arms Great Warley.

66. This 1900 card shows that this rather fine old inn has changed but little over the years, except the horse trough no longer exists. The delivery cart belonged to Pond and Langrish, who had a grocery business next to The Bell in the High Street which many will remember was owned latterly by G.F. Morgan. The sign of the inn Thatchers Arms is extremely uncommon, in fact there are no Thatchers Arms as such; the College of Heralds has never made such a grant of arms.

Golding's Cottages and Tooks Farm, Great Warley.

67. This pretty view of Great Warley Street of 1902 hardly looks like the main road to Tilbury it is today. The cottages were part of the Goldings estate of E. Heseltine, whose beautiful house and grounds across the road has now become the New World Inn and restaurant. The photographer was fortunate to capture in his picture an itinerant knife-grinder, a Mr. Butts who describes himself on his machine as a cutler, who also undertook to repair umbrellas and rivet china and glass. These men were a familiar sight in our streets in the past, but it is now a vanished trade, no one does it any more.

68. Here is another of the many fine houses which abounded in the Brentwood area. This is Coombe Lodge; about a hundred years ago it was one of the more elegant Victorian erections, the beautiful verandah giving it something of a colonial atmosphere. It was occupied latterly by General de Rougement and his family, his son Denys took an important interest in local affairs. It still exists but has now become an hotel. The house is said to have been built for a member of the Ind family which, with the Coope's, founded the famous brewery at Romford and later at Burton-on-Trent. The Coope's lived at Rochetts at South Weald.

Military Funeral leaving Warley Barracks Brentwood.

69. The same London postcard photographer who took view 67 was also lucky enough to capture the unusual spectacle of a military funeral when he reached the barracks at Warley. The cortege is wearing the uniform red of the days before khaki had been introduced and are bearing reversed arms with the right arm behind the back. It has just emerged from the garrison church situated behind the officers mess, which can just be seen on the right, and is on what is now known as Eagle Way, presumably en route to the cemetery at Lorne Road.

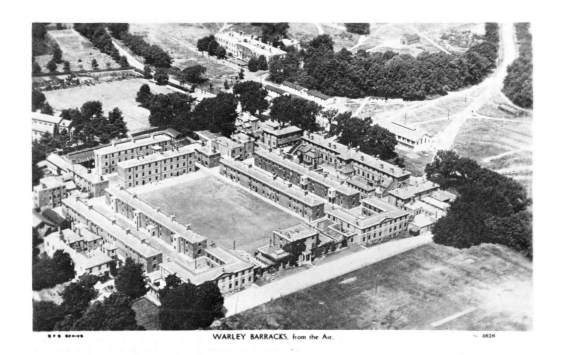

WARLEY BARRACKS, from the Air.

3826

70. This aerial view shows the extent of the former military station which was in two parts: depot Essex Regiment and a Guards barracks; all of which has been demolished with much now being used by the Ford Motor Company. The building with the portico (lower front) was the Guards Officers Mess; the garrison church is extreme upper left, the old married quarters are top centre. The open area right was at one time a race course. The road leading up on the right is now The Drive.

71. Going by the garrison church and Warley Gap, the lane leads to Childerditch Common where is the favourite Greyhound Inn, shown here in a card reproduced from a painting by Basil Holmes before the property was considerably reconstructed some years ago. It has always been a popular place for picnics at week-ends in summer. There was a 9-hole golf course on the common until about fifty years ago.

Thornden Avenue, Brentwood.

72. The Avenue which passes between Harts Wood and Thorndon Park has always been a favourite walk with Brentwood folk. This view looking towards the Running Waters has not changed very materially though some private house development has occured on the Harts Wood side. The Thorndon estate saw-mill was behind the fence on the right, and Lion Lodge is behind the photographer.

73. This card, which is post-marked 1910, shows Woodman Road which appears to have a very rough surface and little paving at this time. The photographer has carefully grouped all those who wished to 'get in the picture'. Little building appears to have yet occured on the right, the former Guardsman public house can be seen left, and a market cart stands outside Mr. Cowling's dairy. Upland Road now branches left by the little shop, and the new Warley cemetery is on the left by the second group of trees.

Brentwood, Seven Arches Bridge

74. Continuing along Hartswood Road which is carried across the very deep railway cutting by the rather fine Seven Arch Bridge, which was built entirely from the bricks of the demolished mansion of Mill Green House at Ingatestone. On the right there was a mail-bag receiving and despatching apparatus in use until the widening of the line. The Great Eastern locomotive is one of Holden's long lived 'Intermediate' class; a hundred were built 1891-1902, some lasting until the very end of steam.

75. This superb postcard of 1902-03 has captured the 'Norfolk Coast Express', pride of the Great Eastern Railway, here thundering up the difficult Brentwood Bank just west of the Seven Arch Bridge. The second engine is one of the new Claud Hamilton class fitted experimentally with the Holden oil-burning apparatus. Notice the oil tank on top of the tender in lieu of a supply of coal. The locomotives are putting up a grand show of steam and smoke as both firemen work hard to maintain a full head of steam.

Cornslands, Brentwood

76. At the time this view was taken in Cornslands (circa 1910) only the first five houses had been built. This is approximately the point where the recent development of Lakeside Crescent and Wren Place join this private road which has never been made up.

77. This rare view must have been photographed from the top of the railway bank near where Upper Cornslands is now located. The high building at the left is Hill's brewery when it was still operating; it was taken over by Ind Coope early this century. It then became the engineering works of Mitchell Brothers for many years. The houses on the right are on the west side of Myrtle Road, those on the east side have not yet been put up. Newly completed houses in Warley Mount just show above the brewery. This area is now all re-developed with Cameron Close covering most of it.

BRENTWOOD, STENFIELD COMMON.

78. This unfamiliar view card, posted in 1904, shows the third pond on Shenfield Common which was known as Burgess's. It was at the foot of the 'tips' but gradually dried out leaving a wet sludgy area. The newly planted avenue of trees along Seven Arches Road can be seen on the left, the house near the centre is facing the mill pond.

The Bandstand, Shenfield Common.

79. This is the elegant bandstand which adorned Shenfield Common many years ago. It stood in the hollow below the mill pond which made a natural arena for listeners. The hollow had been formed by people helping themselves to the good gravel obtainable until the common came under the care of Conservators who introduced some regulation. The view is taken looking east across to Ingrave Road; the avenue leading to Thorndon Park down the centre of the common is visible also.

The Pond, Shenfield Common.   No. 1065

80. This is a 1928 view card of part of the mill pond, so named because two windmills formerly stood on the other side of the road where The Chase is now. All drivers of horse-drawn vehicles took the opportunity to refresh their animals if they were in the vicinity of the pond. This is Mr. Cowlings milk cart at the pond. Behind is a Dodge truck of Mr. Upton, who had a butchers business near the top of High Street, which passed to the London Cooperative Society when he retired.

Brentwood. Shenfield Common.

81. This postcard of 1909 shows the third pond on Shenfield Common. It was made by a schoolmaster at the Grammar School named How, about 1860. For many years it was known as How's Folly. Most of the houses along this part of Ingrave Road were built around the turn of the century with an occasional older one here and there, including a small farm used by a pig dealer for a long time. At some time a railing was placed alongside the pond which has now ceased to exist for some years.

82. Farther along the Ingrave Road is the Fountain Head which was only a tiny beerhouse at the time of this photograph when there were only a few cottages in the area. It is now modernised to meet the needs of the great increase in population on the new estate which almost surrounds it. The fence on the right is part of Mortimers timber yard and saw mill which has traded here for many years. The road appears to be in a shocking state. The public house stands at the meeting point of three parishes: Shenfield, Ingrave and Great Warley.

THORNDON HALL, from the Air

83. This interesting aerial view of Thorndon Hall shows the two subsidiary sections of the hall linked to the main building by curved corridors. The grand portico is on the south front. The hall was severely damaged by a disastrous fire in 1878. The property was never restored, Lord Petre transfering his household thereafter to Ingatestone Hall, which is still the family seat. The present conversion of the property into superior flats will no doubt assist in securing the well-being of this fine house for the future.

84. The north front of Thorndon Hall photographed in its semi-derelict state following the disastrous fire. The curved connecting corridors are clearly seen here. One of the wing sections served as the club house for the Thorndon Park Golf Club which has a fine course in the park. The edifice was constructed to designs by Thomas Paine.

85. This delightful little weather boarded timber built public house stood on the left of the Tilbury Road in Ingrave shortly before reaching the cricket common. It was known as the Maltsters Arms. It was one of Fielders' houses and at the time of the picture the licencee was Samuel Saunders. It was closed as such in the later 1920's.

THE CRICKET COMMON, HERONGATE. 1904.

Fred Spalding
Photo
Chelmsford
Copyright

86. The Herongate cricket common as it appeared on a card of 1908, a very pleasant scene which has not changed very materially over the years. The large residence behind the green is Park House, home of the Rennie family for a number of years. The building on the left in the trees was converted into a motor garage and filling station about fifty years ago.

'The Cricketers' Herongate.

87. Herongate: the main Tilbury Road circa 1914 still looking very much a country lane. The gabled building is the Cricketers public house with its sign board. It closed in the 1920's to become Pardey & Johnsons grocery store. The white boarded building is the post office and left is part of the Peculiar Peoples Chapel which closed a few years ago.

88. A little farther south on the same road as the last view looking towards Brentwood by the road on the left. In the centre is the old village schoolroom, to the right is the Green Man Inn; its sign board can clearly be seen. Herongate House stands in the trees right, and East Horndon rectory grounds are just behind the old signpost, which has clearly been made by a local craftsman.

Brentwood, Middleton Hall & Lane.

89. This card shows Middleton Hall which was the home of Joseph Tasker Esq., and later of his daughter Countess Tasker upon whose death it became a private mental institution conducted by Dr. Haynes, following which it has become the preparatory department of Brentwood School. It was a very beautiful house with fine grounds and a first class stud at the rear. The lane made a pleasant walk near to town centre, but more recently has become heavily trafficked by vehicles avoiding the cross roads, so would not today be very suitable for teaching a lady to ride a bicycle.

The Village, Shenfield   No. 464

90. A 1926 view of the High Road at Shenfield. Right is the forge and wheelwrights shop of the Rayner family, left is Worrin Road, named after the owner of Glanthams Farm nearby, which also gives it name to a road on the estate. Shenfield Place, home of the Courage family, is on the right. A farmer's float is outside the smithy whilst the horse is inside being shod. New development has meant the demolition of these traditional buildings. Notice the very unusual road warning sign.

91. Just below the Shenfield forge stood the parish pump, seen here shortly after it had been renovated after falling into a very dilapidated state about 1927. The old gentleman filling his pail is George Dowsett, who was a familiar figure in the village for many many years during which time he fulfilled the duties of postman. He lived in the cottages across the road. The pump has now vanished with the redevelopment of the area.

92. This view at about 1930 at the junction with Hutton Road shows the Green Dragon Inn, which is still recognisable, and to the right Platt's Garage which was taken down soon after this was photographed. The new premises can just be seen nearing completion behind. Petrol is on sale for 1/4d (6½p) a gallon; the large advertisement of the Parade Cinema tells us that the big films to be exhibited that week were 'Temptation' and 'Rumba'. The usual collection of oil cabinets and similar impedimenta of the period are all there.

SHENFIELD. 1645.
'Eagle and Child'

Fred Spalding.
Photo.
Chelmsford.
Copyright.

93. The camera, now pointed down Chelmsford Road, shows the original Eagle and Child Inn which was always known as the Bird and Baby. It was replaced by the present building about 1936. Shorter Avenue and Tudor Close now branch off right and a motor garage erected where the trees are; there was a little hairdressers establishment just to the right of the inn. The customary horse trough is by the post supporting the inn sign. The present garage in Hutton Road was originally started in the old farm buildings on the left in 1919. There was a good bowling green and club behind the inn until it was taken down.

94. Hutton Road, Shenfield about 1908 when it first began to develop as a residential district. Left is the first parade of shops newly finished with only two yet occupied. Glanthams Farm, mentioned earlier, stands behind the trees on the left, and shops and the parish hall have since been built on the open land on the right. The corn and pet food shop soon changed hands and continued as a butchers shop for a very long time.

95. An interior view of the first Shenfield station in Great Eastern days about 1910. The signal box can be seen at the far end of the down platform. There is an interesting assortment of enamelled metal signs nailed on the fencing which includes Sutton's Seeds, Epps Cocoa, Mazawattee Tea, Bovril, Brands Essence and Walkers Gravesend Ales and Stout, only two of these products can be purchased today. There was one more platform on the right which accommodated the branch train off the Southend line when it did not run through to London. The locomotive approaching is running with the express goods head code.

96. This view of the same date as the last shows the exterior of the station and the small arch over the Rayleigh Road. The whole of the old station buildings were demolished when the railway was widened, so only the older generation will recognise anything here. Shops have now completely covered all the land on the left, and also on the right, compare with the next card.

The L. & N. E. Railway Station, Shenfield.   No. 1502

97. Here may be seen the impressive new station buildings which replaced those shown in the last two illustrations after doubling of the tracks to Shenfield Junction. They show a certain dignity and fitness for purpose. Outside a venerable heavy old limousine long discarded from some gentleman's service waits patiently for its next fare. The aluminium bonneted car to the left is a smart little Rover 9 tourer with hood erected.

'Junction'

SHENFIELD. 1582.

Fred Spalding
Photo.
Chelmsford.
Copyright

98. Passing through the Shenfield station arch to Hutton. This 1906 view is taken at the foot of Bishops Hill facing the arch. Alexander Lane is on the right, and the Hambro office block, which now dominates the scene, is built over the site of Letch's (later Preece & Horn) taxicab garage. The carts outside the Hutton Junction Hotel await their drivers who have stopped 'to water the horses'. It is now simply 'The Hutton', named after a noted geologist James Hutton (1720-1797). All spare land hereabouts is now built over.

The Village, Hutton.
No. 1116.

99. A view of 1929 at Hutton by the Chequers Inn before any new building had started, Cedar Road now branches at the side of the inn, and nothing has yet been built on Collins Farm land in the distance. The milk float is Mr. Cross's of Hutton dairy, an early Westcliff bus approaches on its way to Wood Green. The land on the left is now all part of the London County Council estate.

100. Hutton, a pre-1914 view of the junction of Wash Road (right) with Rayleigh Road in which the main road looks very much like a lane. The buildings in the distance are the residential units of the Poplar Schools. The whole of the land in front has more recently been taken by the London County Council for housing purposes, with shops fronting on to Rayleigh Road. The Chequers Inn, see last card, is on the left just off the picture.

101. The Brentwood Council and its officers in 1922, most of whom served for many years. Standing are Councillors A.G. Collis, an electrical engineer; G.S. Aldridge, saddler; J.F. Hough, headmaster of the Grammar School; H.P. Maynard, draper and furnisher, successor to J.J. Crowe; S. Ruggles, of whom no information; A.J. Meeson, the surveyor; and A.D. Cheshire, the Asst. Clerk. Seated are S. Frazer, medical officer; C.E. Lewis, Clerk, also Coroner; Councillors, S. Vincent, veterinary surgeon; F.W. Bittles, headmaster National Schools; J.T. West, retired; W.A. Wilson of Wilson's stores; and A.J. Gibson, medical practitioner.

102. A line-up of the first motor taxicabs in the town circa 1919-20 on the rank on the 'down' side of Brentwood station, which quickly led to the withdrawel of the horse cabs. The nearest driver is Walter Wood, who was still a taxi-driver thirty years later, the driver at the left is believed to be one of the Hendersons' who ran taxis for some years. All are model T Fords, two of which have left-hand drive. Alexandra Road and the Hunter Memorial Hall in the background.

103. In 1908 a party of intrepid Brentwood licensed victuallers and their friends ventured an excursion by one of the 'new-fangled' motor-buses for their summer outing, Maldon being the destination. The omnibus was hired from Thomas Tilling of Peckham from a batch of Dennis chassis with which it was experimenting. They are about to start from the Railway Tavern with an adequate supply of suitable refreshment stowed away no doubt. Notice that no man is without a hat or cap and almost all sport a button-hole which was considered 'de riguer' on such occasions in those days.

104. An interesting card of a bygone craft of importance during the era of the horse and of the motor until car makers built their own bodies. This is the exterior of the Ellis family business, founded in 1890 in King Edward Road. The forge and wheelwright section was conducted in a building to the left. The staff are here working on the back axle and fore-carriage of a fairly heavy trade cart which can be seen within. The business ceased in the late 1930's.

105. The visit of a travelling fair or circus in the days before television was an event of more than ordinary interest. This card of 1927 shows Nicholl's switch-back gondolas arriving in the town. It is stopped by Roden House in Shenfield Road while the crew take refreshment in Maddison's coffee shop before proceeding to the fair field, whence it would be accompanied by an army of boys and youths on foot or cycle who would eagerly watch its assembly. The train of waggons is being hauled by the magnificent showman's scenic road locomotive 'Queen of the South' built by Burrell's of Thetford, Norfolk.

106. An inside view of the Royal Laundry in Ongar Road soon after it was opened in 1905 by W.F. Saunders (in bowler hat) and his partner and manageress Miss Abbot (the lady in black). The premises have been progressively enlarged over the years, the business now forming part of the Advance group. Observe the quantity of frilled and heavily starched articles, everything is dazzling white, coloured underwear or house linen was virtually unknown at this date.

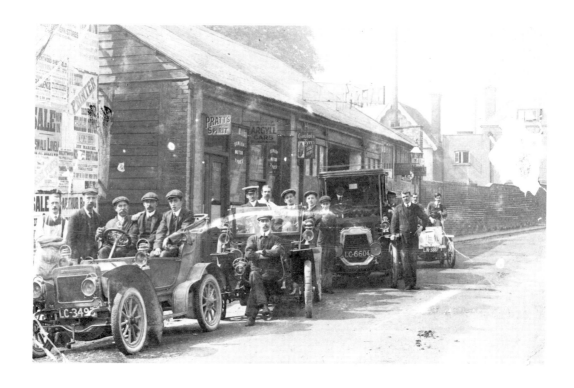

107. This very worn card is of Johnstone Bros' motor garage near the top of Kings Road, circa 1907, which was the birthplace of the motor trade in Brentwood. Here can be seen J. Rolfe, who started in North Road and later at the Mountnessing Motor Works; J.P. Hensmans of Brook Street garage; John Clark of White Hart Garage and Harold Guy of the Ongar Road Quick Service garage, who all received their training here. The premises began as a skating rink, but has now become Bennett's undertaking establishment. Carter Paterson, the carriers, had their depot and stables behind the hoarding.

108. Only older residents will remember when omnibuses like this were in Brentwood. This is one of the independents or 'pirates' which challenged the London General Co's near monopoly between 1924 and 1934 when London Transport acquired them compulsorily. This is The Reliance which ran to Leytonstone where the card shows it taking layover before returning. Others which went to Stratford included the B.B.P., Chadwell, Martin and Atlas. Others ran coaches, the best remembered being Hillman's and Sunset or Victory, which ran to Bow or Charing Cross.